Professional Guide to Macros and Programming in Excel

Author: Rafael Solis

Introduction

Macros and programming in Excel, through VBA (Visual Basic for Applications), are skills that allow you to automate tasks, improve efficiency, and solve problems in a personalized way in a professional or personal environment.
This comprehensive guide will take you from the basics to advanced projects that you can implement in your spreadsheets.

This book is structured so that beginners understand the key concepts, and intermediate/advanced users can explore more complex ideas.
With this guide, you will not only learn to write macros but also to design efficient and scalable solutions.

Table of Contents

Chapter 1: Fundamentals of VBA

What is VBA (Visual Basic for Applications)?

Detailed explanation of the topic: This section delves into concepts with practical examples and clear steps to help you implement macros and related functions.

Code Example:

```
Sub MyFirstMacro()

        ' This code displays a popup message

        MsgBox "Hello, world!"

End Sub
```

Example Explanation: This basic macro uses MsgBox to display a message to the user. It is the first step to understanding how to interact with users through VBA.

Practical Exercise:

Create a macro that asks for the user's name using InputBox and greets them with MsgBox. Example:
- Question: "What is your name?"
- Answer: "Hello, [User's Name]"

The VBA Editor Environment (IDE)

Detailed explanation of the topic: This section delves into concepts with practical examples and clear steps to
help you implement macros and related functions.

Code Example:

```
Sub MyFirstMacro()

        ' This code displays a popup
message

        MsgBox "Hello, world!"

End Sub
```

Example Explanation: This basic macro uses MsgBox to display a message to the user. It is the first step to understanding how to interact with users through VBA.

Practical Exercise:

Create a macro that asks for the user's name using InputBox and greets them with MsgBox. Example:
- Question: "What is your name?"
- Answer: "Hello, [User's Name]"

Macro Structure

Detailed explanation of the topic: This section delves into concepts with practical examples and clear steps to help you implement macros and related functions.

Code Example:

```
Sub MyFirstMacro()

        ' This code displays a popup
message

        MsgBox "Hello, world!"

End Sub
```

Example Explanation: This basic macro uses MsgBox to display a message to the user. It is the first step to understanding how to interact with users through VBA.

Practical Exercise:

Create a macro that asks for the user's name using InputBox and greets them with MsgBox. Example:
- Question: "What is your name?"
- Answer: "Hello, [User's Name]"

Chapter 2: First Steps with VBA Programming

Data Types and Variables in VBA

Detailed explanation of the topic: This section delves into concepts with practical examples and clear steps to help you implement macros and related functions.

Code Example:

```
Sub MyFirstMacro()
```

```
        ' This code displays a popup
message

        MsgBox "Hello, world!"

End Sub
```

Example Explanation: This basic macro uses MsgBox to display a message to the user. It is the first step to understanding how to interact with users through VBA.

Practical Exercise:

Create a macro that asks for the user's name using InputBox and greets them with MsgBox. Example:
- Question: "What is your name?"
- Answer: "Hello, [User's Name]"

Conditional Structures and Loops

Detailed explanation of the topic: This section delves into concepts with practical examples and clear steps to help you implement macros and related functions.

Code Example:

```vba
Sub MyFirstMacro()

        ' This code displays a popup
message

        MsgBox "Hello, world!"

End Sub
```

Example Explanation: This basic macro uses MsgBox to display a message to the user. It is the first step to understanding how to interact with users through VBA.

Practical Exercise:

Create a macro that asks for the user's name using InputBox and greets them with MsgBox. Example:
- Question: "What is your name?"
- Answer: "Hello, [User's Name]"

Procedures and Functions

Detailed explanation of the topic: This section delves into concepts with practical examples and clear steps to help you implement macros and related functions.

Code Example:

```
Sub MyFirstMacro()

        ' This code displays a popup
message

        MsgBox "Hello, world!"

End Sub
```

Example Explanation: This basic macro uses MsgBox to display a message to the user. It is the first step to understanding how to interact with users through VBA.

Practical Exercise:

Create a macro that asks for the user's name using InputBox and greets them with MsgBox. Example:
- Question: "What is your name?"
- Answer: "Hello, [User's Name]"

Chapter 3: Working with Excel Objects

Objects, Methods, and Properties

Detailed explanation of the topic: This section delves into concepts with practical examples and clear steps to help you implement macros and related functions.

Code Example:

```
Sub MyFirstMacro()

        ' This code displays a popup message

        MsgBox "Hello, world!"

End Sub
```

Example Explanation: This basic macro uses MsgBox to display a message to the user. It is the first step to understanding how to interact with users through VBA.

Practical Exercise:

Create a macro that asks for the user's name using InputBox and greets them with MsgBox. Example:
- Question: "What is your name?"
- Answer: "Hello, [User's Name]"

Manipulating Cells and Ranges

Detailed explanation of the topic: This section delves into concepts with practical examples and clear steps to help you implement macros and related functions.

Code Example:

```
Sub MyFirstMacro()

        ' This code displays a popup message

        MsgBox "Hello, world!"

End Sub
```

Example Explanation: This basic macro uses MsgBox to display a message to the user. It is the first step to understanding how to interact with users through VBA.

Practical Exercise:

Create a macro that asks for the user's name using InputBox and greets them with MsgBox. Example:
- Question: "What is your name?"
- Answer: "Hello, [User's Name]"

Managing Sheets and Workbooks

Detailed explanation of the topic: This section delves into concepts with practical examples and clear steps to help you implement macros and related functions.

Code Example:

```
Sub MyFirstMacro()

        ' This code displays a popup
message

        MsgBox "Hello, world!"

End Sub
```

Example Explanation: This basic macro uses MsgBox to display a message to the user. It is the first step to understanding how to interact with users through VBA.

Practical Exercise:

Create a macro that asks for the user's name using InputBox and greets them with MsgBox. Example:
- Question: "What is your name?"
- Answer: "Hello, [User's Name]"

Chapter 4: User Interaction

InputBox and MsgBox

Detailed explanation of the topic: This section delves into concepts with practical examples and clear steps to help you implement macros and related functions.

Code Example:

```
Sub MyFirstMacro()
```

```
        ' This code displays a popup
message

        MsgBox "Hello, world!"

End Sub
```

Example Explanation: This basic macro uses MsgBox to display a message to the user. It is the first step to understanding how to interact with users through VBA.

Practical Exercise:

Create a macro that asks for the user's name using InputBox and greets them with MsgBox. Example:
- Question: "What is your name?"
- Answer: "Hello, [User's Name]"

Forms in VBA

Detailed explanation of the topic: This section delves into concepts with practical examples and clear steps to help you implement macros and related functions.

Code Example:

```
Sub MyFirstMacro()

        ' This code displays a popup
message

        MsgBox "Hello, world!"

End Sub
```

Example Explanation: This basic macro uses MsgBox to display a message to the user. It is the first step to understanding how to interact with users through VBA.

Practical Exercise:

Create a macro that asks for the user's name using InputBox and greets them with MsgBox. Example:
- Question: "What is your name?"
- Answer: "Hello, [User's Name]"

Error Handling

Detailed explanation of the topic: This section delves into concepts with practical examples and clear steps to help you implement macros and related functions.

Code Example:

Sub MyFirstMacro()

        ' This code displays a popup message

        MsgBox "Hello, world!"

End Sub

Example Explanation: This basic macro uses MsgBox to display a message to the user. It is the first step to understanding how to interact with users through VBA.

Practical Exercise:

Create a macro that asks for the user's name using InputBox and greets them with MsgBox. Example:
- Question: "What is your name?"
- Answer: "Hello, [User's Name]"

Chapter 5: Practical Projects

Automating Common Tasks

Detailed explanation of the topic: This section delves into concepts with practical examples and clear steps to help you implement macros and related functions.

Code Example:

```
Sub MyFirstMacro()

        ' This code displays a popup
message

        MsgBox "Hello, world!"

End Sub
```

Example Explanation: This basic macro uses MsgBox to display a message to the user. It is the first step to understanding how to interact with users through VBA.

Practical Exercise:

Create a macro that asks for the user's

name using InputBox and greets them with MsgBox. Example:
- Question: "What is your name?"
- Answer: "Hello, [User's Name]"

Creating a Control Panel with Forms

Detailed explanation of the topic: This section delves into concepts with practical examples and clear steps to
help you implement macros and related functions.

Code Example:

```
Sub MyFirstMacro()

        ' This code displays a popup message

        MsgBox "Hello, world!"

End Sub
```

Example Explanation: This basic macro uses MsgBox to display a message to the user. It is the first step to understanding how to interact with users through VBA.

Practical Exercise:

Create a macro that asks for the user's name using InputBox and greets them with MsgBox. Example:
- Question: "What is your name?"
- Answer: "Hello, [User's Name]"

Exporting Data to Other Formats

Detailed explanation of the topic: This section delves into concepts with practical examples and clear steps to
help you implement macros and related functions.

Code Example:

```
Sub MyFirstMacro()

        ' This code displays a popup
message

        MsgBox "Hello, world!"

End Sub
```

Example Explanation: This basic macro uses MsgBox to display a message to the user. It is the first step to understanding how to interact with users through VBA.

Practical Exercise:

Create a macro that asks for the user's name using InputBox and greets them with MsgBox. Example:
- Question: "What is your name?"
- Answer: "Hello, [User's Name]"

Chapter 6: Optimization and Best Practices

Debugging and Testing Macros

Detailed explanation of the topic: This section delves into concepts with practical examples and clear steps to
help you implement macros and related functions.

Code Example:

```
Sub MyFirstMacro()

        ' This code displays a popup
message
```

```
    MsgBox "Hello, world!"

End Sub
```

Example Explanation: This basic macro uses MsgBox to display a message to the user. It is the first step to understanding how to interact with users through VBA.

Practical Exercise:

Create a macro that asks for the user's name using InputBox and greets them with MsgBox. Example:
- Question: "What is your name?"
- Answer: "Hello, [User's Name]"

Writing Clean and Reusable Code

Detailed explanation of the topic: This section delves into concepts with practical examples and clear steps to help you implement macros and related functions.

Code Example:

```
Sub MyFirstMacro()
```

```
            ' This code displays a popup
message

        MsgBox "Hello, world!"

End Sub
```

Example Explanation: This basic macro
uses MsgBox to display a message to the
user. It is the first step to understanding
how to interact with users through VBA.

Practical Exercise:

Create a macro that asks for the user's
name using InputBox and greets them with
MsgBox. Example:
- Question: "What is your name?"
- Answer: "Hello, [User's Name]"

Avoiding Common Problems

Detailed explanation of the topic: This
section delves into concepts with practical
examples and clear steps to
help you implement macros and related
functions.

Code Example:

```vba
Sub MyFirstMacro()

        ' This code displays a popup
message

        MsgBox "Hello, world!"

End Sub
```

Example Explanation: This basic macro uses MsgBox to display a message to the user. It is the first step to understanding how to interact with users through VBA.

Practical Exercise:

Create a macro that asks for the user's name using InputBox and greets them with MsgBox. Example:
- Question: "What is your name?"
- Answer: "Hello, [User's Name]"

Chapter 7: Additional Resources

Useful Libraries and References

Detailed explanation of the topic: This

section delves into concepts with practical examples and clear steps to
help you implement macros and related functions.

Code Example:

Sub MyFirstMacro()

    ' This code displays a popup message

    MsgBox "Hello, world!"

End Sub

Example Explanation: This basic macro uses MsgBox to display a message to the user. It is the first step to understanding how to interact with users through VBA.

Practical Exercise:

Create a macro that asks for the user's name using InputBox and greets them with MsgBox. Example:
- Question: "What is your name?"
- Answer: "Hello, [User's Name]"

Extensions and Add-ons

Detailed explanation of the topic: This section delves into concepts with practical examples and clear steps to help you implement macros and related functions.

Code Example:

```
Sub MyFirstMacro()

        ' This code displays a popup message

            MsgBox "Hello, world!"

End Sub
```

Example Explanation: This basic macro uses MsgBox to display a message to the user. It is the first step to understanding how to interact with users through VBA.

Practical Exercise:

Create a macro that asks for the user's name using InputBox and greets them with MsgBox. Example:

- Question: "What is your name?"
- Answer: "Hello, [User's Name]"

Advanced Practical Projects

Automating weekly financial reports.

Detailed description of the project, steps for implementation, and relevant code snippets.

Consolidating data from multiple sheets into a summary.

Detailed description of the project, steps for implementation, and relevant code snippets.

Creating interactive forms for data entry.

Detailed description of the project, steps for implementation, and relevant code snippets.

Automatically generating charts and exporting them as PDFs.

Detailed description of the project, steps for implementation, and relevant code snippets.

Integrating Excel with Word and Outlook for automated reporting.

Detailed description of the project, steps for implementation, and relevant code snippets.

Additional Resources

- Recommended Websites: Official Microsoft Documentation, Stack Overflow forums.
- Recommended Books: "Excel VBA Programming for Dummies".
- Useful Add-ons: Power Query, Power Pivot, and advanced Office tools.

www.ingramcontent.com/pod-product-compliance
Lightning Source LLC
Chambersburg PA
CBHW030046230526
45472CB00005B/1696